The Dear Remote Nearness of You

Danielle Legros Georges

The Dear Remote Nearness of You

Danielle Legros Georges

Barrow Street Press
New York City

Cover Photo: Gerard Georges

Published 2016 by Barrow Street, Inc.
(501) (c) 3) corporation. All contributions are tax deductible.
Distributed by:
    Barrow Street Books
    P.O. Box 1558
    Kingston, RI 02881

Barrow Street Books are also distributed by Small Press Distribution,
SPD, 1341 Seventh Street Berkeley, CA 94710-1409, spd@spdbooks.org;
(510) 524-1668, (800) 869-7553 (Toll-free within the US); amazon.com;
Ingram Periodicals Inc., 1240 Heil Quaker Blvd, PO Box 7000,
La Vergne, TN 37086-700 (615) 213-3574; and Armadillo & Co., 7310
S. La Cienega Blvd, Inglewood, CA 90302, (310) 693-6061.

Special thanks to the University of Rhode Island English Department and
especially the PhD Program in English, 60 Upper College Road, Swan
114, Kingston, RI 02881, (401) 874-5931, which provides valuable
in-kind support, including graduate and undergraduate interns.

First Edition

Library of Congress Control Number: 2016933721

ISBN 978-0-9893296-9-9

CONTENTS

I

II

III

IV

Acknowledgements

Notes

I

I will steal I will steal
The orbit of the savage moon
The meagre sobs of the waves
Arriving from the other shore
Joyce Mansour

If blues, then

bring in a dog;
someone done
profoundly wrong,

a kitchen, two women
talking, a man and
a woman talking,
he lost, 3,000 miles

away. Fetch some
red clay, a steady rain;
leave wearing one
boot and a shoe,

that's how bad.
A shine-eye girl,
a boy running from
the law. The law

itself. A man called
a *fellow*, a woman
called *my girl, my baby,
my gal.* You a stone,

a mule. A bend
in the road, the load
too heavy, Lord, yes
the Lord. The crossroads,

a packet of roots, twigs,
a figure in the dark
waiting near a light
but you can't get there.

A seamless pattern of
stumbles and stops,
roadblocks.
A red dress

left hanging in a closet,
a pair of pants with nothing
in its pockets. The world

conspiring to add
to whatever's riding
you. The dust in
the air settling slowly.

The Easter *Rara*

Port-au-Prince

Again the noise comes, an approaching concatenation
from around Delmas, an afternoon clatter, then the *rara* itself,
earthbound and utterly: plinkety-plink of grey spoons

on glass bottles, yellow bass bamboo trumpets, instrument
bosses of repeating hiccups who won't be undone by the *guiras'*
brush on the silver downbeat. *Rara* of intermittent maracas,

music of call-a-politician-a-name-but-you-can't-prove-it.
The lyrical *yes* to all that needs a *yes* to; and between
the *abas*, "down with," some dazzling thief of a legislator;

the high cost of living; whatever's grinding you to red dust.
And the *rara* gets loose, gets low, gobbles all in its way: a stray
goat sucked into the whirl gets spun around, gets taken down.

* * *

Restaveks offer the *rara* the dark cocoons of their child-servant lives.
The human mass cradles them as their parents did not,
as their upper-class, middle-class masters do not. Let the *rara* take

their beatings. Let the *rara* beat it all purple. Let them be reborn
to the beauty of unblinking good fortune, to the accidents of riches,
to the deep crimes of wealth. Let the *rara* bear witness to new life,

and hard life, and no kind of life at all. Let the *rara* pound the earth,
pulse through town, storm cloud of the *majòjon*, wielding a baton,
leading the *rara* on.

7

We Eat Cold Eels and Think Distant Thoughts

Said American boxer Jack Johnson, glistening like a fish,
    To the newsman who asked him why white
        Women were drawn to black men, like him.

What is it like to eat cold eels and think distant thoughts?
    What is it like to be a *black man* who eats cold eels
        And thinks distant thoughts? What is it like to be

A black man who thinks to say we eat cold eels and think
    Distant thoughts to a white reporter, early-1900s America,
        Who wants to reduce him to meat, to red, to sexual.

Once in the Chicago Aquarium, a long time ago,
    I met an eel I was told by the label on his large
        Tank weighed 53 pounds and was 100 years old.

It looked at me with such a fierce intelligence through the glass
    And silty water of its address—its grey bald head almost human,
        Its two lidless eyes, its small nose holes—and instead of a body

Below its head, no body but a tail of fluid form, one great muscle
    Behind ears that were not ears, but also holes. Its whole body
        Beating a slow chilled rhythm that kept it afloat.

And a cool terror shot through me, as it watched me watch it,
    As it followed me through the liquid wall that split our worlds,
        And separated our species.

Still Life with Orbs

Between the thing
and the name of it,
is a world,
and a world
behind this world.

There is my mask
placed on the table.
There is the wooden
table and the space
beneath it. There
is an orange on the floor
when it should
be on the table

in the yellow basket
meant for oranges
but which contains a cat,
licking one front paw.

What do cats know
of oranges? What do
birds know of water
unless they plunge
their beaks into it
breaking some poor
fish's sleep. What do
fish know of birds
except the slash of bill,
the sudden flash,
the stop.

The Paper Map

The newspaper scrolls the morning by.
This black-and-white world unfurls its terms:
A clear face, wiped of its features,
fades into a blank night; an uprising
in a bordering town; a *black-on-black*
crime of uncountable skulls that
flower in whiteness—and whiteness.
What creeps into the body and wants
to dig its way out?

How do we dissolve?

The shutter flickers. All goes black.
The morning shatters in its cage.
The hood stays put, and the body
covered, arms outstretched,
is a hanger of wires. A wooden box
holds the weight of a man.

How does he stand?

The photo will not reveal the time.
The footage will not disclose the spot.
The victims will not be returned
to states of unknowing.
The victims will not be returned
to the page of before this.

Poem from the Real World

Boston

I'm on Dorchester Ave. when I hear it: *nigger*. It is
September 28, 2004, and I haven't heard the word used
this way in so long I'm for some seconds stunned, and
simultaneously amused in the way an archeologist might be,
coming upon the grotto of some long-extinct tribe she's been
studying for years, to discover their swear words etched in the
cave. And almost in the same moment I say to myself *He's
not talking to me,* and keep walking. It's a temperate, lovely
day: Indian summer (*Indian summer* asterisked for further
study), blustery, and again it comes: *nigger.* And nigger
comes creeping, slowly, from his coffin: fettered, measured,
lynched and raped, reconstructed, redlined, incarcerated,
deconstructed and resurrected (I would have preferred *negress,*
more charming and belle-lettristique, more gendered, past the
purpose and grasp of the wielder of *nigger*—but I digress, and
return to the task of inscription with what is available to me,
that is, language). There is no poetry here because there is no
poetry here. I am recording this to remind myself this wasn't
an odd dream—the result of having watched one too many
PBS documentaries on Civil Rights and race relations in the
United States, of imagining a young Linda Brown crossing
the train switchyard to school, Topeka, Kansas, 1952. I am
recording this to remind myself that this did indeed happen
on September 28, 2004, in Boston, Massachusetts, the
U. S. of A.

As Falling Star

The impossible task of breathing
      Near guns, breathing and running,

Breathing and standing as still as
      Death when it closes you off,

When it wraps its arm around you.
      If breathing is living, if breath is

Spirit, what spirit lifts you off
      The earth?

Death, see your
      -Self here as fear.

As falling stripe. As falling
      Star.

Poem of History

When living your life, you are not *making history*.
Stepping out of your life, you make of it, history.

Jamal, doctoral student whose city apartment
I've sublet, has gone this summer to Egypt to write

A story, which is and is not history, gone before
Egypt exploded in history: Its leader pulled down

Like a kite by his people; Jamal in the *foule*,
In the crowd, as it opens its flag of history:

Not amber but action, a lamp glowing in shadows
Of history, like the light of my lamp on Jamal's

Table-turned-desk on which I write history,
His apartment blurred in the heat of summer.

White octagonal tiles and a claw-foot tub govern
The bathroom. I draw water from the waters

Of history, cool and safe from the blood of history;
I draw water from the sink of the kitchen, cool

And clear, for the lilies standing bright as stars
On the table by the white wall and window.

Outside the grey buildings past the green plaisance,
The university sprawls like a beast. How lovely

Its lawns, its evening lights. Patrolled by dark
Guards drawn from the dark city periphery,

An irony not lost on them, in inky corners
Posted, shielding the denizens of the university

From others like them. Inside and out. The confines
Of safety. The black jungle. The grey jungle.

The towers, the lush avenues, the colossal
Structures. The sources of knowledge.

A dark flower. A guarding of history.

Carson Beach

Boston

Spring arrives all caution, a cat that smells
something suspicious—its brown paws testing
the snow-fighting-for-its-life, and the earth
beneath it all, knowing snow's jig's up.

The sky lifts its gunmetal grill, decides
it no longer wants to hold the sun captive
and would rather have it a convict on the lam.

Seagulls who know no shame crap
into the shifting sea, which forgives them
and cleans up their mess, small crest
by small crest.

This sea is not reckless like the Caribbean,
which blinds you with its blue sheen.
This sea is unruffled. It doesn't sit
or leap, exactly, but ripples its cool.
It flexes. It purrs.

Praisesong for Boston

Begin with the Massachusett, setting nets in the harbor
Of Boston, before it was *Boston* harbor—*Quonehassit,*
Place of clear water, and arrive at my door. I, immigrant

Like so many settlers nestled in your arms, write this poem
To you, Boston. If I write *Trimount*, it is for your hills,
Some still standing, others razed, the land changed, as lands are,

As time passes, and yet history is yours, Boston, the good and bad of it,
The inarticulated and the often-stated: A Puritan's beacon, Wheatley's
Pen, Winthrop's city upon a Hill, Walker's Appeal to the Coloured

Citizens of the world, the vision and grandeur that are Gardner's,
The words lost to the grey-and-blue Atlantic. If I place an emerald
Necklace at your feet, it is to match the medallions of your ever-turning

Wheels: bicycles and schoolbuses, the railroads and helms of trade
And fate, of fire and grit, of determination's grip, of cod and beans,
And the great house of science, and the great house of knowledge,

And the great house of art. International since the day you were born,
If cities are born. And if you are grown, then out of everything you
Have grown: a revolution's spark, the arc of a wide bridge,

Cable-stayed, lit electric, wharves and new waves,
And the complicated notions of freedom and forward,
And the ease of summer days and sturdy neighbors:

Chris, young terror of Sumner Street; Alana eating a pear,
Already in third grade; John, but call him Mac; Santiago
Who yells louder than God; and Wendy who yells louder;

And Wayne, uncle to all, from his big yellow house greeting
Each newcomer to the neighborhood.

The Flowers Mr. Miranda Planted for his Dead Wife

What to do with the bloody dahlias
in Mr. Miranda's yard? Jutting over
the fence, they bludgeon passersby

with their beauty. Rotund, red, so dark
in their red to be violet. Undeniable ladies.
Why so merciless? Why force us to stop,

to wish to leap into your fragrant arms
at first light when we should be thinking
other things, muted things:
pale roses, the most guiltless,
guileless pink.

II

Living is no joke
Nàzim Hikmet

Bright Field

My echolocation: left—
Not a direction
but a lack.

And so, and so, I
skim-float, undeft
bat in day-

light. Blind as blind
is, lost in light's
field,

flapping, flappably
tackling all by
feel,

bumping into what
is, and what is
real,

into what tells me
where I am.

Intersection

Haiti 2010

The earth shook. A portal opened.
I walked through it. The earth shook.
A portal opened. I walked through
it. The earth shook. A portal opened.
I walked through it. The earth shook. A
portal opened. I walked through it. The
earth shook. A portal opened. I walked
through it. The earth shook. A portal
opened. I walked through it. The earth
shook. A portal opened. I walked through
it. Ash. The earth shook. A portal opened.
I walked through it. Earth. The earth shook.
A portal opened. I walked through it. Ash.
The earth shook. A portal opened. I walked.
The earth shook. A portal opened. I walked
through it. Through it. I walked. The earth shook.
A portal opened. I walk through it. The earth
shook. A portal opens. I walk through it.

In the Next Town

What about such gravity makes us
want to live? Pulled
from the rubble:

A woman in ash. A boy who carries
his broken-armed sister
down a hill.

What in us says *life*. Life.
Life after 20 days
entombed.

Life in the singing at the door, not
even a door, the
remains,

the imprint

of a church. The Lord somehow,
Jesus, somehow. Mother Mary
somehow.

All the gods descendant.
The gate. The gate.
The crossroads

and the light. How does a country
bury its too hastily
buried dead?

A Credence

The prison. The real cell.
The bars of one's own
making. The scars, and flesh
beneath still quaking.

The dire need to breathe.
The stars and sky on fire.
Seed and pyre. The turning,
turning all to dust. The air.

A hole bored through
a tent's blue ceiling.
The sky reeling.
Reeling.

Will. Force. The weight
that will not let you die.
A million, million, million
whys. An absence

of antecedents. A frankness.
A tension. A craggy flower,
rough blossom, repeating.

For the Poorest Country in the Western Hemisphere

You should be called beacon. You should
be called flame. Almond and bougainvillea,
Garden and green mountain, villa and hut,

girl with red ribbons in her hair,
books under arm, charmed by the light
of morning, charcoal seller in black skirt,

encircled by dead trees. You, country,
are merchant woman and eager clerk,
grandfather at the gate, at the crossroads

with the flashlight, with all in sight.

Why Lalane Did Not Go to Haiti in 2009

Cholesterol, high blood pressure, glaucoma,
two laser surgeries. In October: cataracts.
Complications, complications, I tell you,

I could find good doctors, yes, of course,
but if the hospitals don't have things, *chuut!*
Even blood you'd have to buy, even needles.

If I'm there for two days, OK, but you don't
know if the *tension* will come for you—
or the coma. *Et les kidnappings!*

These days, the place is finished. Finished,
mes amis.

You Will Listen to Me—1

New York: A man who built a voodoo shrine using his
ex-girlfriend's underwear—then killed her mother, and
a dog—was sentenced Thursday to 28 years to life in prison.
The ex-girlfriend, Françoise McDaley, 16, told police that
Pierre Carrenard, 36, harassed her after she broke up with
him. On the day of the crimes, it is reported Carrenard called
her at work and threatened her mother, Esperance Labidou,
a Haitian immigrant who worked at a bus company.
Carrenard later stabbed the mother 25 times in her home
before he turned the knife on her Chihuahua, Foo Foo. He
then fled to Florida. Police found a shrine in his apartment
made of McDaley's underwear and one of his socks tied
together with a vine. Carrenard explained in court that the
shrine "was a sort of spell to control her spirit." Police also
found a letter in his apartment: All I want to do is to love
you and make a life with you, but your family keeps getting
in the way. Let this be the last interference. You will no
longer listen to your family. You will listen to me.

You Will Listen to Me—2

What you have just read is a condensed
transcript of a real news story, "Man
with voodoo shrine gets life in prison."

No byline accompanies our titillating tale
of murderous love; the wild pair of sock
and underwear, vine of love; the breed

-ID'd dog, whose name in Creole sounds
like "Crazy Crazy." What is crazy? The man
stabbing the mother; the man knifing the dog,

the story itself a dog rummaging for a bone.
And what of the girl? Only 16 to the man's 36.
Here the story doesn't blink. Should we write

a new headline, leave voodoo alone, and continue
to climb up this story's vine? "Man with mental
illness menaces family." Do not leave me, dear
reader, as I dredge up the details, the facts.

A Dominican Poem

If you are born, and you are stateless,
if you are born, and you are homeless,

if your state and home are not
yours—and yet everything you know—

what are you? Who are you? And who
am I without the dark fields I walk upon,

the streets I know, the blue corners
I call mine, the ones you call yours . . .

Who am I to call myself *citizen*, and
human and *free*? And who are you

to call yourself landed and grounded,
and free. And who is judge enough?

Who citizen enough? And who native?
Who other?

And who are we who move so freely
without accents of identification,

without skin of identification, with
all manner of identification. With

gold seals of approval. With stamps
of good fortune. With the accident

of blameless birth. Who are we to be
so lucky?

Lingua Franca with Flora

In spite of all who would renounce petals
the petals come: *chèlbè* some, shy some,
no dirt will hold them back. Planted
in dirt, and drawing from dirt, they explode
hot pink, burst red, blown clean in the trade
winds that sweep down like a Moorish lover;
washed clean, darkened by Caribbean Sea rain:
these creeping bougainvillea.

And hibiscus flower, still delicate, still fleshy,
returning constantly to the Haitian day
he was stripped like a god of his name:
Rose de Chine. To the day he was brought low
to blacken shoes, made to show his black blood
in the shine on the boots of American Marines,
1915. He who, now named *choublak*, spills
his dark tears for tea.

But who can deny the sly *chevalier de nuit*?
Night's knight, who blooms only at night,
unbolting his tiny white flower, perfumed,
redolant. Intoxicant known to those
who travel the night, and the night into day
down the worn trails to town, down the hills
for something, for life; known to those who
cut deals with ominous lords, with the devil
himself. All pinned by his lance.

It is he this girl picks to sweeten her dress
as she *will* emerge a goddess in a rinsed
azure shift, after birdbath in alley
with enamel tin cup and tan bucket.
She will go boldly to her love who will
whisper to her in a schoolboy French
learned before he quit school, before life
swallowed him—and to seal their accord
(for there *is* a deal being made) in the gravity
of Creole, *wi cheri, wi, tout sa'm genyen se pou ou,*
yes darling, yes, all I have is yours.

III

Here is the room with closed doors
Ida Faubert

A Poem to Be the Poem That Was

winding itself down a dark alleyway
when dusk was most dusk and threatening
day with never returning.

A poem becoming a subtle mother,
a sweet and mean keeper
and breaker of bones.

A poem to be a hospital to medicate
a malady out of a lime body,
out of blue veins.

When this poem finally utters its name,
flames also utter theirs,
a copper pot boils over,

a sputter shivers and draws a blank,
a blanket just won't do for cover.

Lesson

Romulus and Remus, twin sons of Mars, set adrift on the River
Tiber as toddlers, had been suckled and tended
by a she-wolf. This is a fact

I learned. This is a legend, a sanctioned item brought forth
by Sister Celestine in the grey light of Latin class.
Romulus slew Remus for having leaped

over a wall, a stone line of demarcation, and though a killer,
carried by his father, god of war, protector of fields,
to heaven, and deified by the Romans.

Remus, if he has his own entry in the encyclopaedia,
is forever tied to his brother. The dark she-wolf,
mysterious, compelling,

could be seen roaming the wide field of the text; the bellicose
roaming the world; the nuns directing
as best they could

what they could not explain away. Order is something else
I saw: what came first, what followed, the inaudible
fall-in, the tuck

of sameness. How else to explain the legion we girls
became in our navy jumpers and serious
blouses, in the heavy shoes

we tied on each morning. How else to counter the fine hair
that grew on our bellies.

Love Spell No. 6

They say if you wake wet in the night
The devil's been visiting you. How else

To define your grip on the bedpost,
The steam your thighs give to the room's

Eyeless heat, though blame the pepper
In the red stew if you want to, the meat

Marinating by the kitchen's cool
Counter. To catch a man

All a girl's got to do is place the steak
She's fixing to feed him between

Her legs when she's bleeding. Give that
To him for a love so fierce he'll murmur

"Sweet Jesus"

Then forget about God.
The Lord has nothing to do with this.

Egg

after Linda Pastan

Darling, you are an egg. There is no in, there is no
out. The germ of you remains embraced. To free
you would be to break you, to spread you over the
black face of a heat, to eat you. Then you would
travel through me, through throat and entrails
to earth—to the body of the earth, becoming
more than you've ever seen, more
than you've ever known.

Arc

A lizard skitters across the pavement like a line
across a page.

Its meter trochaic, its demeanor grave. Green
scale, green scale.

Break. A shift like a blink. A sunray illuminates
its almost-mind,

the mind we were, you and I, a unison of armor,
a sidle and gleam.

The city: Cold and brilliant. You, inarticulately
beautiful.

The restaurant whose name we never could
remember

in order to give it new names we could
remember.

Our winter sun that flashed and fell.

Broad Wing

I want to disable desire, to free roaring in me something
Inchoate and large as the world. As a girl I lay in bed

Rubbing the big and second toes of my right foot together
In a slow meditation, in an endless act, back and forward,

Slow and forward, forward and back, and for some reason,
By some physics I do not understand, I would feel myself

Lift close to the room's ceiling, and my toes become two
Planets, rubbing their extraordinary masses together,

And the two planets more massive than anything I could
Comprehend, in the darkness that I knew was the universe,
infinite.

What this has to do with sadness, I don't know, except
as a small silver river and some way to return to my body,

this page, which is a way to stay the broad wing of sadness,
which seems linked to desire, the longing for what

Can't be re-seen, be re-felt, what can never be direct again.

The Dear Remote Nearness of You

for Patrick

Across the space you seem
To pixelate a dream, a breakage
And a screen, your simulacrum

Since the last I held you fast
En chair et en os, one
Joint against the next, your

Hand soft on my neck, your
Clavicle and chest, my breast
Against your breast.

Like this three years have passed,
Like water, air, like glass,
On dusty roads, in planes,

On mountaintops, and me against
The you I thought you were, and you
against your sense of me,

And finally, and still, and yet
Some space above it all
For falling free, while somehow tied

A knotted two, a ribbon, a small
Boat on the ocean. The wood,
An oar and open sea.

Love Spell No. 8

I will watch you watch me.

I will be the faintest beat, the tannest

Shade of heart, a pulse imperceptible.

If your house has a middle post, I am it.

If your lake ripples only once, I am

The sand grain dropped in it.

Willing

Should there be a shift
In the weather.

Should a thunderbolt
Expose its fierce arm to us.

Should the past and present
Clash, birth some other

Sense of being.
Then yes, build me a city.

I will scale its walls.
Survey its hills.

Read all the books there are.
Lick every vat of cream.

Heat milk till it's frothy,
Then flat, then float in it.

Only

Nature hides
the most beautiful

design: the norm,
the anomaly,

the rare, the rarest,
which is to say,

the only, and aren't we
each, twins even, only?

IV

In whose language
                    Am I
                    Am I not . . .
Marlene NourbeSe Philip

Light Thief

I delight in dust and dimness. Slim as a suggestion,
    I slip up the light-post to brightness, slip a snare
round its neck, send it sputtering down.

I rip the gleam. Archangel. My crime and making:
    one. As a beauty queen takes all shimmer,
to dimmer spots I'll go with it.

I'll fill a light bulb hung over a rough cradle,
    shake a shadow from pure pitch, tunnel
like a long-tail rat, make the darkness wail,

make you see what the hell you're doing,
    what the hell you're in: all roaches and cat,
all people and dead dog. I'm the deep turned

demimonde. I'm the black turned blue.
    I'm a shift in mood. The trash floating
in the spit of the sea, I light it, yeah,

that's me: your outlaw connection
    to sight, your free no-charge vision,
your 30-watt shantytown glow.

Train

This train is built only to move us,
you and me. Its fliers would have us
buy this type of crème to straighten hair,
have this doctor exfoliate the dead
cells from our faces, making each
a perfect star. We riders do not
gaze at one another, but eye our feet,
read our headlines. They bleat what we
ought to know when we emerge
from the ground: a man
flattened by police, an increase
in violent crime that's taken the city
hostage. No passenger can move.
No matter. This is the metropole.
A child's high voice screeches across
the hum and stumble of wheels,
through the announcement *Spring
Street* and the dull razor of metal doors.

Elegy for Tim Johnson

Tim Johnson, you are dead
though we spent Christmas together
many years ago.

You bought me an extravagant Swiss
coffeemaker that was much too much
for where we were in our never-to-be.

I never used it, gleaming thing that burps
and groans discharging its silvery steam,
until now. Tim, you are dead. I'm left

to sort out what this means. You were always
on the edge of becoming the next big thing
except I knew you wouldn't be—you did

more talking of becoming than becoming.
Still that's no reason you should be gone.

Had you heeded your body. Had the sugar
in your blood broken down as it should
have, been sucked fiercely into your cells.

Had you seen your hunger and thirst
as more than hunger and thirst—not been
the black man alone when your heart

failed you, alone on a gurney in the worst
emergency room of the worst hospital
of the biggest city in the world.

You are gone, Tim Johnson,
and I hardly knew you, and what I did
know of you did you no good.

Landscape in Violet

Dream of dim smoke and cigarettes, a mouthful
of clouds. Distract the teeth from your jaw.
Draw a long sip with a lanky straw.

If you're a fish and wish to breathe, sift
the water in brightly through the gills—
your orange tail flickering, a ballgown, a flame.

If not, be slow, believe the water air. Don't shout.
Be the tree felled in the blue woods. Be the no one
around. Be the frozen ground calling the trunk.

How Else

How else to say that rape is used as a weapon
Of war *but rape is used as a weapon of war.*
Your child who runs in a verdant field.

The one who knows the god-awful nature
of her name, and the face of her mother
which is her face, and the face

Of hate and the face of love.
Another image: A child born as children
Should come, into the world's calm hand,

Into its sun. The sun is not silent.
How else to say that rape is used as a weapon.
It wasn't from any desire . . . The only answer I have

is they wanted to destroy me; to kill my spirit.
The spirit separates, lifts from body and returns.
The spirit separates the living body from the corpse.

A child separates the dying from the future.
The death dealers flee. This child looks
The future in its face.

Binary Death

To say *death is death*
is to raise metaphor's shadow—
from the dead would not be good, so
from some dark, so from some dark

       leap from unlike to unlike
a deepening—not frying pan
and fire, but fire and then none.

None being the opposite
of whatever. The there
and the not. Knotted two,
once double,
once both,
once once.

Instances of Blue

This blue is deliberate, a move from the red, into something else. To night and what it means. To the unruffled and to ruffling. Ink and keys. To speed. Expression is the antidote to repression. So be it. As it is written. So it is done. So it is written. So it is done. Neither over. Nor under. Toward the temperate. Blue more somber. A constellation's backdrop. A darkness against light. Black's sister. Spare. The one between navy and aquamarine, with green. And aquamarine: a bath, a sea. A sky: its quality of never-ending forevering, and everything. A robin's egg. Danger blues. The maps of the world. The new maps. Blood through the flesh before it pours out of the body. The blues, of course, of course. Lady sings. Women singing. Through and away the blues. My grandmother's belts worn beneath her peacock dress. Her devotion to pale Mary, mother of all mothers, and to the inky Erzulie, also Mary and more. Underneath it all. To the beauty of letters on blue paper. And when there is no paper, to that beauty too.

Pleasant Street, Spring

With spring on my back, around my neck,
with the clock turned forward, into breaking
open slowly, onto muted skyscape,

into dusk-flight, dogwood, dangerously careening
blossom, flesh-flare of leg on sidewalk walking,
into fern, green stone, grass, tree, one more word

and I will be swimming in a garden. And now:
verdigris. There it is. What to say, what to say
but give me the world. Wonder too. Force

me a line, force me in line with what's
around me, off this page. Drop the space
between this and there. There.

Still Life in Green and Violet

in response to Georgia O'Keeffe

The black lily with its black heart juts out of the green
lettuce of the world, insisting on itself, asking for your eyes.
Yet the flower keeps its secret: a half-shielded bullet,
a singular heart. O curtain of green billows, o vulval patterns,
o frippery of white. Black lily: You are not black at all, but
a violet saturation. A sweet slash of black holds you up on the
right, and on the left red, red—but not so red as the inner
folds. *Erotica.* This is *erotica*: Jack in the Pulpit as oyster,
Jack in the Pulpit as black pearl. The inner heart of the body,
and less the body whole, seen from outside. The heart speaks
its own language and is not the heart at all. Above you, lily,
shines a light. Above it all, a far-off light. Like a god-light.
An unfolding speaks of *revelation*. Which is another word for
admission; disclosure and permission. Primordial dark matter
rendered in violet. All this is a mask. What I want to talk
about is loneliness, but that would reveal too much. Who
would want this mass and make it glow?

I Want You

For your back, I want you, for the ease.
For your form I want you, your mind free
so to please only me. For your hands and your feet
and sweet slack I want you, for your easily identified
black I want you. For years I want you, for years
And more years, and your life I want you.
For your kind I want you. For all time
I want you. It's a crime I want you. At times
don't know when, don't know how I want you.
In a line I want you. For what's mine I
want you. For science, and art, and what's
fine I want you. Yes indeed, yes indeed,
I want you.

Acknowledgments

Grateful acknowledgment is made to the editors of the following journals and sites in which these poems first appeared, some in slightly different versions:

Bill Moyers Journal program and website: "For the Poorest Country in the Western Hemisphere"
Boston Public Library website: "Praisesong for Boston"
BreakWater Review: "Instances of Blue," "Still Life in Green and Violet"
Callaloo: "If blues, then," "The Paper Map," "Still Life with Orbs," "Lingua Franca with Flora"
The Caribbean Writer: "A Credence"
Ibbetson Street: "Why Lalane Did Not Go to Haiti in 2009," "Carson Beach"
Mass Poetry website: "A Dominican Poem"
Poiesis: "Poem from the Real World," "Intersection," "In the Next Town," "Bright Field," "The Flowers Mr. Miranda Planted for his Dead Wife"
Proud Flesh: "The Easter *Rara*," "Light Thief"
Salamander: "Lesson," "Egg," "Arc"
Solstice Magazine: "A Poem to Be the Poem That Was," "Elegy for Tim Johnson"
sx salon: "You Will Listen to Me"
spoKe: "How Else," "Binary Death," "I Want You," "Landscape in Violet"
Transition: "We Eat Cold Eels and Think Distant Thoughts," "As Falling Star"
Tuesday: An Art Project: "Pleasant Street, Spring"
World Literature Today: "The Dear Remote Nearness of You," "Only"

Thank you Patrick Etienne, Corinne Adler, Colette Brésilla, Grace Cambridge, Afaa Michael Weaver, Martha Collins, Richard Hoffman and Kathi Aguero, Harris Gardner, Charles Coe, Elizabeth McKim, Ilda St. Jean, Mary Buchinger, Nadine Pinède, Patrick Romain, Jean-Claude Martineau, and Zanset Yo.

Special thanks to the Massachusetts Cultural Council, the City of Boston Mayor's Office of Arts and Culture, the William Joiner Institute for the Study of War and Social Consequences, Lesley University, the Writers' Room of Boston, and the Boston Foundation.

Notes

Lines of Joyce Mansour's which open the first section are drawn from her poem "Of Sweet Rest" translated from the French by Mary Beach.

Line of Nâzim Hikmet's which opens the second section is drawn from his poem "On Living" translated from the Turkish by Randy Blasing and Mutlu Konuk.

Line of Ida Faubert's which opens the third section is drawn from her poem "Halt" translated from the French by the author.

Lines of Marlene NourbeSe Philip's which open the fourth section are drawn from her poem "Meditations on the Declension of Beauty by the Girl with the Flying Cheek-bones"

"You Will Listen to Me—1" and "You Will Listen to Me—2" draw from the news story *Man with Voodoo Shrine Gets Life in Prison* by the Associated Press, August 18, 2006.

"A Dominican Poem" addresses a September 2013 ruling by the Dominican Republic Constitutional Court that stripped citizenship from Dominican-born people without a Dominican parent, going back to 1929. The majority of people affected are Dominicans of Haitian descent.

"The Easter *Rara*" references *rara*, a type of festival music played in street processions in Haiti.

"Lingua Franca with Flora" contains *chèlbè*, Haitian Creole for *showy* and "American Marines, 1915," a reference to the 1915–1934 U.S. military occupation of Haiti.

"Light Thief" borrows a line from Edward Baugh's "The Warner-Woman" which appears in his volume *It Was the Singing*.

"A Bedtime Story" draws from a 2008 UNICEF report and the words of girls and women who survived sexual violence in the Democratic Republic of the Congo.

Danielle Legros Georges is poet, writer and professor at Lesley University. In 2014 she was appointed Poet Laureate of the City of Boston, a position in which she acts as an advocate for poetry, language and the arts, and creates a unique artistic legacy through public readings and civic events. She also teaches in the Joiner Institute for the Study of War and Social Consequences Writer's Workshop, University of Massachusetts, Boston. She is the author of a volume of poems, *Maroon* (Northwestern University Press, 2001) and articles, essays, and reviews in the areas of Caribbean literature and studies, American poetry, and literary translation. Her poems have been widely anthologized.

Photo: Priscilla Harmel

BARROW STREET POETRY

You Have to Laugh: New + Selected Poems
Mairéad Byrne (2013)

Wreck Me
Sally Ball (2013)

Blight, Blight, Blight, Ray of Hope
Frank Montesonti (2012)

Self-evident
Scott Hightower (2012)

Emblem
Richard Hoffman (2011)

Mechanical Fireflies
Doug Ramspeck (2011)

Warranty in Zulu
Matthew Gavin Frank (2010)

Heterotopia
Lesley Wheeler (2010)

This Noisy Egg
Nicole Walker (2010)

Black Leapt In
Chris Forhan (2009)

Boy with Flowers
Ely Shipley (2008)

Gold Star Road
Richard Hoffman (2007)

Hidden Sequel
Stan Sanvel Rubin (2006)

Annus Mirabilis
Sally Ball (2005)

A Hat on the Bed
Christine Scanlon (2004)

Hiatus
Evelyn Reilly (2004)

3.14159+
Lois Hirshkowitz (2004)

Selah
Joshua Corey (2003)